LUCIA,
SAINT OF LIGHT

BY KATHERINE BOLGER HYDE

WITH ILLUSTRATIONS BY DARIA FISHER

ANCIENT FAITH PUBLISHING
Chesterton, Indiana

LUCIA, SAINT OF LIGHT

Text copyright © 2008 by Katherine Bolger Hyde
Illustrations copyright © 2009 by Daria Fisher

Published by
    Ancient Faith Publishing
    P.O. Box 748
    Chesterton, IN 46304

Printed in Canada

ISBN 978-0-9822770-4-1

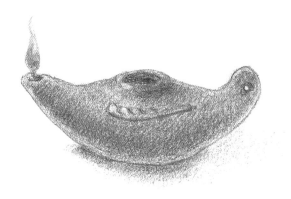

To Nektarios & Anna Burkett,
who first introduced me to St. Lucia
—Katherine Bolger Hyde

To family, without whom we are nothing
—Daria Fisher

Today is my nameday! My name is Lucy, and this is December 13, the Feast of St. Lucia. It's one of my favorite days of the year.

On this day, I wake up early, before it's light. My sisters and I put on long white gowns trimmed with lace. Kirsten and Ingrid are my attendants; they wear sashes and wreaths of tinsel. I'm the Lucia bride, so I tie my gown with a wide red ribbon. On my head goes a crown made of lingonberry leaves that holds seven candles. When I put it on, I feel like St. Lucia herself, come to bring light and joy to the dark winter land.

In the kitchen, I make a pot of coffee and pour it carefully into
a blue-and-white china coffeepot my mother brought from Sweden. I
put the coffee things on a tray with a plate of ginger cookies and special
cross-shaped sweet buns called Lussekatter—Lucia cats.

My sisters help me, but my brothers Lars and Carl are too
busy goofing around, using their star-boy hats for helmets
and jousting with their star poles. "Hush!" I tell them. "You'll
wake Mom and Dad!"

When everything is ready, I hold the tray and lead the procession. We parade into my parents' bedroom and wake them up, singing a song about St. Lucia.

Then we all sit on the big bed, munching "cats" and
gingerbread and singing Christmas carols. We're all so cozy,
I wish this part of the day could last forever.

But the rest of the day is fun too. When my parents are dressed, we go next door to visit Mrs. Sundstrom. We bring her coffee and cat buns and sing to her as well. When we finish she has tears in her eyes. She always says to me in her thick accent, "When I vass a young girl in Sveden, I vass da Lucia bride. You make me feel like a little girl in Sveden again."

Then my mother sits on the bed and talks to Mrs. Sundstrom in Swedish for a while. I guess they're probably talking about Sweden.

I've never been to Sweden, but my mother grew up there. She was a Lucia bride when she was a girl, too, and when she came to America and married my father she brought the tradition with her.

Once, when I was younger, I asked her to tell me about St. Lucia and why we celebrate her the way we do.

"Well, it's kind of a peculiar story," my mother said. "You see, St. Lucia isn't actually a Swedish saint. She was born in Sicily, an island off the coast of Italy.

"Back when St. Lucia was born, in the late third century, Sicily was part of the Roman Empire. Lucia's father was a wealthy nobleman, but he died when Lucia was a baby. Her mother raised her to be a Christian."

"But wasn't it against the law to be a Christian back then?" I asked.

My mother smiled. "You've been paying attention to the saints' lives in church, haven't you? Yes, it was against the law. Christians had to hide their faith, or they risked being arrested, tortured, and put to death. You had to love God very much to take that risk.

"Lucia grew up loving God with all her heart. She loved Him so much that she didn't want to marry anyone but her heavenly Bridegroom, Jesus Christ. But her mother, Eutychia, didn't understand this, and she arranged for Lucia to marry a man who was a pagan.

"After this, Eutychia became very ill. Lucia persuaded her mother to go on pilgrimage with her to St. Agatha's tomb. There Lucia had a vision. St. Agatha appeared to her and told her God was pleased with her desire to remain a virgin.

"Eutychia was healed, and Lucia begged her mother not to force her into marriage, but to let her give her dowry away to the poor instead. In those days a girl could not be married without a dowry."

"Like the girls in the St. Nicholas story!" I said. "St. Nicholas left money in their stockings so they could get married."

"That's right. Well, after a while, Lucia's fiancé heard that she and her mother were giving all their money to the poor. He wasn't happy about that at all. In fact, he was so angry that he went to the governor of the island, Paschasius, and told him that Lucia was a Christian.

"Paschasius had Lucia arrested and brought before him. He commanded her to sacrifice to the idols, but she of course refused. She said she had given everything she owned as a sacrifice to Jesus Christ, and now she was ready to offer her life to Him as well.

"But when the soldiers tried to take her away to torture her, the Holy Spirit made her so heavy she could not be moved. They tried pulling her with ropes, even tying her to several yoke of oxen, but nothing could make her budge from the spot.

"Then, in a rage, Paschasius ordered that she be burned. The soldiers piled wood around her and lit the fire. But Lucia prayed to God, and the fire did not so much as singe a hair on her head. She only glowed with a holy light through the flames.

"Finally, one of the soldiers drove his sword into her throat. Lucia said one last prayer, then gave up her spirit into the hands of her heavenly Bridegroom. She was buried with honor and became the patron saint of her city, Syracuse."

I snuggled closer to my mother. The story was scary, but it gave me a warm glow inside to know that I was named for such a brave and holy girl.

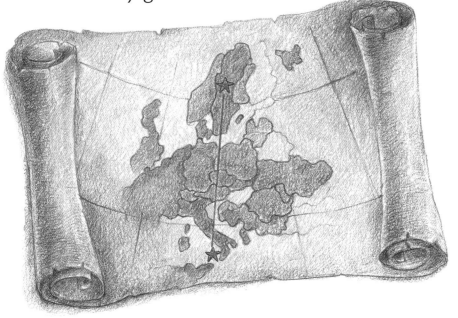

But I was still confused. "If Lucia is the patron saint of Syracuse, how come they celebrate her in Sweden?"

"The Swedes love St. Lucia because she saved Sweden from a terrible famine. Back in the Middle Ages, the people of southern Sweden were starving. On the darkest day of the most terrible winter of all, they saw a boat sailing toward them across Lake Vännern."

"One of those Viking boats with a dragon on it?"

"I suppose so. But instead of a dragon's head at the prow, there stood a beautiful maiden, dressed all in white and glowing with an unearthly light. The people stood amazed as the boat glided toward the shore, with no wind and no oars to propel it, no man at the tiller to guide it. And when the boat reached land, St. Lucia handed out huge sacks of wheat to all the people until the boat was empty. The people would have bread to eat all winter long."

I sighed happily. My saint was not only brave but kind as well. "Is that why Lucia brides wear candles on their heads? Because she was glowing in the boat?"

"Partly that. There was also a legend that Lucia used to visit Christians hiding in the catacombs. In order to keep her hands free to carry the food she brought them, she wore candles on her head.

"That legend might have started because the name Lucia comes from the Latin word for 'light.' Also, her day falls in the darkest part of the winter. In Sweden, the winter nights are very long indeed, with only a few hours of daylight. So St. Lucia came to be associated with the return of the light."

My mother smiled. "Any more questions, my curious Lucy cat?"

I thought for a minute. "Why do we wear white dresses?"

"Because St. Lucia was the bride of Christ. And the red sash is a symbol of martyrdom."

"And we go to visit people like Mrs. Sundstrom because St. Lucia went to visit the poor and the prisoners."

My mother gave me a squeeze. "That's right."

"What about the Lucia cats?" I asked.

"They symbolize the wheat she brought in the famine. And they're shaped like a cross—"

"Because St. Lucia was martyred for Christ! But where does the coffee come in?"

My mother laughed. "That's just because Swedes love coffee."

She sipped from her steaming mug to prove it. I took a cat bun off the heaping plate on the coffee table and thought about all the people St. Lucia had fed. "Mom, can we take these buns over to the Luboviches? I bet they don't get treats like this very often."

She kissed the top of my head. "That's a wonderful idea, sweetheart. And we can sing for them, too."

SANTA LUCIA

by Katherine Hyde,
based on traditional Swedish lyrics

Traditional Neapolitan

Verses from Aposticha for the Feast of St. Lucia:

With what wreaths of praise shall we crown Lucy, the namesake of light? What diadem of honor befits the brow of her who willingly gave up her life for her heavenly Bridegroom, bringing Him as dowry, as though they were priceless rubies, the drops of her precious blood, shed by the sword for His sake?

Come, you who love the martyrs, and let us fashion wreaths of praise, glorifying her who in her pure virginity, her blameless life and spotless death glorified above all the Holy Trinity, the one true God, and put to shame the mindlessness of the pagans! For having been faithful to Christ unto the end, she has truly entered into the joy of her Lord, and abides forever in the eternal bliss of His mansions on high.

Icon of Saint Lucy, courtesy of the Convent of Saint Elizabeth, in Etna, California. The icon is from the wall of the nave of their chapel; mounted copies are available for purchase (http://www.conventof saintelizabeth.org).

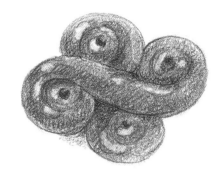

Lussekatter
(Lucia Cat Buns)
(makes 10–12 buns)

1/4 teaspoon saffron threads	5 cups all-purpose flour
8 ounces (1 cup) milk	1 teaspoon salt
1 tablespoon yeast	1/2 cup sugar
1/2 cup sugar	2 large eggs, beaten
4 ounces (1 stick) butter	1 beaten egg white for egg wash

- Using a mortar and pestle, pound saffron threads to break down strands.
- In a small saucepan, heat milk to lukewarm. Mix yeast with 1/4 cup milk and 1 tablespoon sugar. Set aside.
- On low heat, melt butter in saucepan with milk. Add crushed saffron. Let cool.
- In large bowl, mix together flour, salt, and remaining sugar.
- Stir yeast into cooled milk mixture. Mix into dry ingredients, beating to mix well. Add beaten eggs. Knead in bowl for 5–7 minutes. Turn onto floured board and knead another 7–8 minutes.
- Put dough in lightly greased bowl, turn to coat all sides, cover and put in warm, draft-free place to rise for about 1 hour.
- When dough has risen, knead lightly to push out air and divide into small pieces (about 10–12). Using the hands, roll each small piece into a strip about 8–10 inches long. Shape each strip into an "S" or a figure 8. Cross one strip over another to make a cross-shaped bun. Place on lightly buttered cookie sheets.
- Cover with clean cloth and let rise again until double in bulk, about 1 to 1-1/2 hours.
- Preheat oven to 375°F.
- When dough has risen, brush lightly with egg white. Bake in preheated 375° F oven for 15 minutes, or until lightly browned. Let cool on wire rack.

from http://www.fisheaters.com/customsadvent6a.html

Resources

Here are some resources you may wish to consult to learn more about St. Lucia or to assist in planning your St. Lucia celebration.

Websites

http://en.wikipedia.org/wiki/Saint_Lucy%27s_Day
http://en.wikipedia.org/wiki/St._Lucy
http://www.eldrbarry.net/mous/saint/luciaday.htm (includes lots of links)
http://www.squidoo.com/santalucia
http://www.catholic.org/saints/saint.php?saint_id=75
http://www.ewtn.com/library/MARY/STLUCY.htm
http://www.penitents.org/lucy.html
http://www.antiquespectacles.com/topics/patron_saints/saint_lucy/lucy_text.htm
http://www.schooloftheseasons.com/lucy.html
http://www.fisheaters.com/customsadvent6a.html
http://saints.sqpn.com/golden136.htm
http://www.ehow.com/how_7719_celebrate-st-lucia.html
http://www.wf-f.org/stlucy.html
http://www.pasht.net/scandinavian/Lucia.html
http://familyfun.go.com/recipes/special/feature/famf1202_feat_braided/
http://web.tiscali.it/arachne/wink/lucia.htm
http://www.angelfire.com/cantina/homemaking/december13.html
http://www.catholicculture.org/culture/liturgicalyear/activities/view.cfm?id=949
http://www.goarch.org/chapel/saints/635
http://www.monasteryicons.com/monasteryicons/Item_St-Lucy_418_ps_dpr.html
http://www.allmercifulsavior.com/icons/Icons-Lucy.htm
http://www.conventofsaintelizabeth.org/byzicons/print/print.html

Books

Kirsten's Surprise: A Christmas Story (American Girls Collection) by Janet Beeler Shaw
Lucia, Child of Light: The History and Traditions of Sweden's Lucia Celebration, by Florence Ekstrand

About the author & illustrator

KATHERINE BOLGER HYDE is the editorial director for Ancient Faith. She is the author of *The Dome-Singer of Falenda*, a fantasy for ages 10 and up, the adult traditional mystery series Crime with the Classics (Minotaur), and the picture book *Everything Tells Us about God* (Ancient Faith, 2018). She lives in the redwood country of California with her husband and the youngest of her four children. Visit her on the web at www.kbhyde.com.

DARIA FISHER was born in Moscow, Russia, in 1980 and immigrated to the United States with her family in 1991. She holds a BFA in Illustration from Fashion Institute of Technology and presently participates in various disciplines of visual art, including graphic design and iconography. Daria is influenced by the Russian artists of the nineteenth century, masters of the Italian Renaissance, and Art Nouveau. Her work can be viewed online at www.dariafisher.com.